Table of Contents

ii

Background of the Study

General David H. Petraeus stated during his retirement ceremony:

As our nation contemplates difficult budget decisions, I know that our leaders will remember that our people, our men and women in uniform, are our military, and that taking care of them and their families must be our paramount objective.

Beyond that, it will be imperative to maintain a force that not only capitalizes on the extraordinary experience and expertise in our ranks today, but also maintains the versatility and flexibility that have been developed over the past decade in particular. I do believe, however, that we have relearned since 9/11 the timeless lesson that we don't always get to fight the wars for which we are most prepared or most inclined.[1]

Petraeus's remarks at his retirement ceremony were more than casual spoken words. He sent a message warning of a potential "hollow force" similar to the one he found himself in upon graduating from the United States Military Academy in 1974. "I know I speak for many when I say that we came away from that period vowing to never let our forces get to such a point ever again. . . . In the ensuing years, determined leaders transformed what was described as "the hollow Army" and our exhausted military."[2] His comments highlight the requirement to maintain our resources and that future threats may not always align with how we train. Following the Vietnam War, Army Chief of Staff, General Edward C. Meyer introduced the term, hollow force, during a House Armed Committee hearing.[3] Meyer spoke:

Right now, as I have said before, we have a hollow Army. Our forward-deployed forces are at full strength in Europe, in Panama, and in Korea. Our tactical forces in the United States are some 17,000 under strength. Therefore, anywhere you go in the United States,

---

[1]General David H. Petraeus, "Military Farewell Retirement Address" (American Rhetoric Online Speech Bank, delivered 31 August 2011, Arlington, VA), http://www.americanrhetoric.com/speeches/davidpetraeusretirementspeech.htm. (accessed 22 August 2012).

[2]Ibid.

[3]Stephen Daggett and Andrew Feickert, *A Historical Perspective on "Hollow Forces"* (Washington, DC: Congressional Research Service, 2012), http://www.fas.org/sgp/crs/natsec/R42334.pdf (accessed 22 August 2012).

except for the 82nd Airborne Division, which is also filled up, you will find companies and platoons which have been zeroed out.[4]

Meyer's hollow force referred to the shortfall of personnel within the Army; however, the evolution of the hollow force definition has involved personnel, equipment, weapons, and training, which all are elements of military readiness.

Since 1980, when Meyers created the term hollow Army, people and institutions continue to scrutinize military readiness in order to determine whether the military is prepared to conduct its wartime mission. Congressional Oversight committees require that service chiefs provide military readiness status reports. Additionally, service chiefs provide to these committees possible explanations for low military readiness reports, as entailing which factors lead to the lack of military readiness, and possible near and long-term solutions to repair the lack of readiness.

A January 2012 article from the Congressional Research Service exemplifies the origins of a hollow force and provides two periods that evoked the hollow force term. These two periods were post-Vietnam and the 1990s.[5] The research demonstrates the variables concerned (personnel, operational tempo, and funding for weapons programs) were different from one another but both led to outcries of a hollow force.[6] The definitions of a hollow force during these two periods differed from one another. Today, authors continue with this distinction of having different meanings of hollow forces.

During the post-Vietnam era, quality personnel were the main concern because the government introduced the all-volunteer force following the Vietnam War in 1973. "The early years of the all-volunteer force witnessed a significant drop in education levels and test scores among recruits, widespread recruitment scandals, and increases in bad discharges and peacetime

---

[4]U.S. Congress, House of Representatives, *National Defense Funding Levels for Fiscal Year 1981: Hearing before the Investigations Subcommittee of the Committee on Armed Services*, 96th Cong. 2nd sess. (Washington, DC: Government Printing Office, 29 May 1980), 18.

[5]Daggett and Feickert, *A Historical Perspective on "Hollow Forces,"* 2.

[6] Ibid.

desertions."[7] The transition from the draft army to the all-volunteer force took time due to the opposition of "ending the draft."[8] Additionally, "salaries did not keep up with high levels of inflation during the remainder of the 1970s and fell progressively further and further behind the cost of living.[9] Complicating matters, "benefits for military families, such as housing and moving allowances, also lost value, both relative to inflation and in proportion to base pay, making it relatively more difficult for service members with families to make ends meet."[10] Lastly, "shortages, of critical equipment, equipment repair, and availability of repair parts were also recurring apprehensions."[11]

Following the first Gulf War (1991), the U.S. military "was no longer a 'hollow force' by virtue of its performance."[12] However, the "Clinton Administration announced plans to trim $60 billion over the five years through FY1997 from the outgoing Administration's defense plan."[13] In contrast to the post-Vietnam factors, the decline of money provided a sketch of new considerations concerning the hollow force concept. The concerns to the Chiefs of Staff when asked by Senator McCain were as follows:

1. Preserving a high operational tempo at the expense of equipment overhauls and depot maintenance, keeping personnel deployed for excessive periods, and strains on major combat equipment.

2. Increasing depot maintenance backlogs.

---

[7]William Darryl Henderson, *The Hollow Army* (New York: Greenwood Press, 1990), xi.

[8]Robert, K. Griffith, *The US Army's Transition to the All-Volunteer Force 1968-1974* (Washington, DC: Center of Military History, Unites States Army, 1997), 26.

[9]Daggett and Feickert, *A Historical Perspective on "Hollow Forces,"* 3.

[10]Ibid., 4.

[11]Ibid., 5.

[12]Ibid., 10.

[13]Ibid.

3. Underfunding of personnel pay and benefits, inadequate end-strength, and excessive turbulence in personnel deployments.

4. Underfunding of weapons modernization, including upgrades of current systems and purchases of munitions.

5. Funding peacekeeping and humanitarian operations at the expense of readiness.[14]

McCain argued that although the U.S. military was ready to fight, "we took months to adjust the organization, training, and support structures of our armed forces. . . . Without the months Saddam Hussein gave us, these readiness problems might well have cost us thousands of lives. Few future opponents are likely to give us the most precious gift of modern war: time."[15]

With attention to the above concerns, what factors create a hollow force after prolonged combat operations?[16] This question is the purpose of this study. Resources and money are always intermingled, and leaders must decide how to allocate funds to acquire, or maintain, enough resources. According to an article from the Congressional Research Service, "funding decisions played a large role in the overall decline in readiness."[17]

These decisions may lead to a hollow force, which may not be capable to accomplish its assigned missions. In a *National Journal* article, James Kitfield looked toward the next step, to

---

[14]Senator John McCain, "Going Hollow: The Warnings of Our Chiefs of Staff," July 1993, in *A Historical Perspective on "Hollow Forces,"* ed. Stephen Daggett and Andrew Feickert (Washington, DC: Congressional Research Service, 2012), http://www.fas.org/sgp/crs/natsec/R42334.pdf (accessed 22 August 2012), 11,

[15]Ibid., 12.

[16]There is no agreed upon definition of "hollow forces" in literature. There is a concern associated with "hollow forces," Can "hollow forces" complete the assigned mission? This concern blends together discussions of unit readiness and "hollow forces" as seen in the Congressional Budget Office, "Trends in Selected Indicators of Military Readiness, 1980 Through 1993" (Washington, DC: CBO Papers, March 1994), http://www.cbo.gov/sites/default/files/cbofiles/ftpdocs/48xx/doc4888/doc13.pdf (accessed 22 August 2012).

[17]McCain, "Going Hollow: The Warnings of Our Chiefs of Staff," 11.

assign the blame for decreased readiness.[18] This paper will not look to assign blame, but rather illustrate that the decreased resources available after extended combat, caused a change in the military readiness.

As Meyer referenced how the forces "have been zeroed out," similarly military readiness encompasses Meyer's concerns. Military readiness is fundamental to the United States because military forces allow flexible options to the government when negotiating favorable conditions, not only to the United States, but also to other regional countries. The government uses the military in roles such as peacekeeping, deterrence, and combat. In order for the United States to maintain a global bargaining chip, the military must prepare so that at a moment's notice it will complete the assigned mission.

Organization of the Study

The organization of this research study is presented in 5 sections. Section 1 includes the background of the study, statement of the problem, purpose of the study, and significance of the work.

Section 2 presents a literature review while providing a critical overview of current literature on military readiness. Relevant doctrine and the model that will guide the analysis will also be discussed within this chapter. Lastly, the author will identify the variables used in the case study.

The third section will justify the qualitative case study methodology used within the study and identify any possible cases. The author will provide the selection criteria and identify cases examined in the study. Lastly, the scheme for measuring variables will be presented.

Section 4 provides an introduction and narrative for each case study selected. Additionally, the author will show the measured variables, both dependent and independent. In

---

[18]James Kitfield, "The Hollow Force Myth," *Government Executive*, 14 December 1998, http://www.govexec.com/federal-news/1998/12/the-myth-of-the-hollow-force/5300/ (accessed 22 August 2012).

summary, a table will illustrate the results of the chosen case studies by dependent and independent variables.

Finally, section 5 will discuss conclusions and observations during the analysis of the case studies. Additionally, the author will provide recommendations on how to improve upon military readiness.

Literature Review

Amplified by the recent decisions to slash the budget of the Department of Defense following almost 12 years of war in Afghanistan and Iraq, several authors have published literature about hollow forces. Some authors advise caution to military and civilian leaders who guide the armed forces through a period of hollowness, while others cast aside the term hollow forces indicating that people use this term as a buzzword in order to retain money allocated for services or projects. With the recent history of the American military dominating the battlefield, how can a hollow force be present? This study will shed light on questions such as this.

Themes represented in literature correspond to the divergent and convergent thoughts and beliefs related to a hollow force. Due to a lack of shared agreement in the definition of a hollow force, authors continue to disagree about whether a hollow force exists, or if a hollow force is fiction. The text below will provide a summary of the authors' points of view as well as the variables, including both intervening and independent, used in the literature that compare and contrast the causes of hollow forces. Additionally, the author will discuss the model he will use throughout the study, and finally explain the variables used to measure within each of the case studies.

Personnel

Manning is a variable consistent with arguments of a hollow force. Retired Colonel William Darryl Henderson, in his book *The Hollow Army: How the U.S. Army is Oversold and Undermanned*, discusses how the decline of manpower, personnel, and training decreases readiness. He argues that the U.S. Army does not have enough quality or quantity of manpower to mass at a decisive point against an enemy force. According to Carl von Clausewitz, "The first rule, therefore, should be: put the largest possible army into the field. This may sound a platitude, but in reality it is not."[19] Although Henderson's point of having enough manning is valid, he overlooks that bringing mass upon the enemy is not the number of troops, but rather the affect from those troops and weapon systems combined. Therefore, a combination of fewer troops with superior weapon systems can achieve the same effect of mass that Carl von Clausewitz refers to in *On War*, years ago.

Another advocate that military readiness decreases with the decline of manning is Mr. Charles Bloomer who wrote an article, "America's Hollow Military." "Since the end of the Cold War, our forces have been cut in half, cut 35 percent since the Gulf War. The Army has been cut from 18 active divisions to 10."[20] He raises an additional concern regarding the transformation "to a lighter more mobile force."[21] However, the reduction in the number of forces did not change the structure of the force, only the quantity. The Department of Defense already has a smaller (manned) force that conducts rapid missions, the Marines. He mentions his concern regarding a change in force structure. If the Army becomes more mobile, who will fight with heavy equipment like tanks?[22] The purpose of a smaller force is sound because the military should be prepared to fight quickly and "avoid a six-month buildup that was required to get people and equipment in place for Desert Storm." As noted above from Senator John McCain, "Few future opponents are likely to give us the most precious gift of modern war: time."[23]

---

[19]Carl von Clausewitz, *On War*, trans. and ed. Michael Howard and Peter Paret (Princeton, NJ: Princeton University Press, 1976), 195.

[20]Charles Bloomer, "America's hollow army," posted 10 April 2000, http://www.enterstageright.com/archive/articles/0400military.htm (accessed 22 August 2012)

[21]Ibid., 1.

[22]Bloomer, "America's hollow army."

[23]"Going Hollow," Tab A (the report is not paginated; the quoted passage is on the next to last page of the initial section of the report), in *A Historical Perspective on "Hollow Forces,"*

A study, "A Historical Perspective on 'Hollow Forces,'" conducted by the Congressional Research Service illustrates how personnel issues continue to lead to a hollow force: "As pay and benefits eroded over the course of the 1970s, a growing shortage of qualified recruits was directly reflected in assessments of unit readiness. By 1979, the Army fell 15,000 short of its recruitment goal."[24] Pay allocated to personnel was simply insufficient. "By 1980, base pay had declined almost 20% in real terms (adjusted for inflation) since the end of FY1972. Catch up pay raises of 11.7% in 1980 and 14.3% in 1981 narrowed the gap, but were not enough to close it, in part because of the high levels of inflation continued in those years."[25]

Additionally, compounding the issue of manning, are retention and recruiting due to the booming economy during the late 1990s. Bloomer remarks, "In 1999, about 13,000 military families received food stamps and 8,200 received state-supported child-care assistance. Even among more skilled mid-level ranks, the lure of better paying jobs with more desirable working conditions in the civilian sector is tempting."[26] Quality service members must make decisions that support themselves and their families. As one can perceive, there are many factors that affect the variable of personnel within a potential force or hollow force.

Operational Tempo

A different variable, which relates to manning, is operational tempo. The American Enterprise Institute, Foreign Policy Initiative, and The Heritage Foundation released a joint project "Defending Defense Warning Hollow Force Ahead! The Effect of Ever More Defense Budget Cuts on U.S. Armed Forces." In this article, the authors cite a fact, "As recent U.S. military commitments outside of Afghanistan and Iraq have shown, the pace of operations is

---

ed. Daggett and Feickert (Washington, DC: Congressional Research Service, 2012), http://www.fas.org/sgp/crs/natsec/R42334.pdf (accessed 22 August 2012).

[24]Daggett and Feickert, *A Historical Perspective on "Hollow Forces"* (Washington, DC: Congressional Research Service, 2012), http://www.fas.org/sgp/crs/natsec/R42334.pdf (accessed 22 August 2012), 5.

[25]Ibid., 3.

[26]Bloomer, "America's hollow army."

likely to remain high. President Obama has maintained every foreign policy commitment set by his predecessors and added to the military's missions . . . started a new operation in Libya, sent troops to Japan and Haiti for disaster relief operations, and kept 1,200 National Guard troops at America's southwest border."[27] With a smaller future force, continuing these many deployments with a reduced force after prolonged years of combat will potentially decrease military readiness for future situations.

Mr. James Kitfield counters the operational tempo variable in a *National Journal* article, "The Hollow Force Myth." Kitfield states, "all of the major players share the blame for the perceived readiness woes" referring to the Joint Chiefs, the Clinton Administration and the Republican majority at that time.[28] Furthermore, people do not understand "military readiness or unreadiness" which "lies in the eye of the beholder."[29] Kitfield addresses operational tempo citing how Air Force Captain Christopher DeColli and his C-130 aircrew are becoming "tired" due to the high number of flights conducted "that serve as the lifeline for virtually every overseas military operation."[30] Air Force Captain Bly Blaser and his C-130 aircrew counter DeColli's view while interviewed during a flight to Bosnia. Blaser enthusiastically believes in his missions. "What other job lets you take 80 of your closest friends and their luggage on the road with you, and you get to land on short runways and throw 20,000 pounds out the back of your aircraft?"[31]

---

[27]American Enterprise Institute, Foreign Policy Initiative, and The Heritage Foundation, "Defending Defense Warning Hollow Force Ahead! The Effect of Ever More Defense Budget Cuts on U.S. Armed Forces," 21 July 2011, http://www.heritage.org/ research/reports/2011/07/defending-defense-warning-hollow-force-ahead (accessed 22 August 2012).

[28]Kitfield, "The Hollow Force Myth."

[29]Ibid., 2.

[30]Ibid., 4.

[31]Ibid., 5.

These different views illustrate how the viewpoint "lies in the eye of the beholder" and operational tempo is not a factor of readiness or unreadiness.[32]

Additionally, the article by the Congressional Research Service states, "the effect of repeated deployments of forces in military operations abroad became a focus of concerns about readiness. The U.S. military intervention in Haiti in 1994, military operations in Bosnia and Kosovo from 1995 through 1998, and the maintenance of no-fly zones in Iraq from 1993 on, along with a number of other humanitarian operations, were seen as a strain on the force."[33] These deployments caused units to focus on other missions in lieu of their wartime mission.

"Ready for what?" Kitfield asks in his article "The Hollow Force Myth." [34] One rarely discusses the threat or adversary because of the difficulty anticipating what will happen. No one can always predict which enemy will attack the United States or her interests as evident from the terrorist attacks on the World Trade Towers on 11 September 2001. The analysts and Pentagon planners developed the strategy: "prepare, respond, shape" in the 1997 *Quadrennial Defense Review*.[35] "They meant to prepare for the future through modernization; respond to current threats by readiness to fight two major-theater wars nearly simultaneously; and shape the international environment with forward deployments, coalition exercises, military-to-military contacts, port visits, and various other activities designed to stave off crises" or simply stated, "Ready for everything."[36] Although, this 1997 *Quadrennial Defense Review* indirectly called for a review in current force structure in order to fight two major-theater wars nearly simultaneously, the force structure did not increase.

---

[32]Ibid., 2.

[33]Daggett and Feickert, *"A Historical Perspective on "Hollow Forces."*

[34]Kitfield, "The Hollow Force Myth," 6.

[35]Ibid.

[36]Ibid.

Readiness

Mr. Richard Betts in his book, *Military Readiness Concepts, Choices, Consequences*, also discusses military readiness during peacetime. He states that people judge readiness on three facets: "*how much* capability and what elements of it should be available *by what time*" and finally "readiness for what."[37]

"How much" capability refers to the amount of forces in terms of manpower, capable units, and firepower (principle of mass already mentioned) that one can apply against an objective or an adversary. Betts regards the "first task in gauging readiness for what is to identify the enemy against whom military plans must be developed and forces deployed."[38] He refers to "by what time," as how fast units deploy to a region for combat or for their assigned mission. The difficult and most challenging piece to readiness, Betts regards, as the mission or "ready for what." Units must be prepared to accomplish any task. Unit Commanders must make choices as to which task they train more extensively for, in order to be more prepared. Betts requires that readiness must encompass both "speed and effectiveness."[39] Military readiness of units is vital to U.S. national security and global interests.

Another author who discussed the element of, ready for what, is T. R. Fehrenbach in *This Kind of War: A Study in Unpreparedness*. Fehrenbach provided a narrative of the Korean War, in which he revealed that the mission was too large for a Regimental Combat Team. Consequently, after General MacArthur requested, in addition to the Combat Team, he added to "build up later into a two-division force as needed. Over the teletype, MacArthur reiterated that the authority he already had, to put troops into the Pusan area, would not fulfill the mission."[40] MacArthur

---

[37]Richard K. Betts, *Military Readiness Concepts, Choices, Consequences* (Washington, DC: The Brookings Institution, 1995), 35.

[38]Ibid., 36.

[39]Ibid., 38.

[40]Fehrenback provides examples with General MacArthur's cable, "The only assurance for the holding of the present line, and the ability to regain later the lost ground." Additionally,

anticipated the need for additional forces because the existing Regimental Combat Team did not equal enough resources for the assigned mission, a lack of numbers.

Additionally, Dr. Betts discusses, "readiness has often been used in two senses, one too broad and one too narrow."[41] In his book, *Military Readiness Concepts, Choices, Consequences*, he attempts to focus readers on the true concepts of readiness. He notes, "When experts discuss readiness among themselves, rather than with laymen whose interests lie in general policy implications, their usage of the term tends to be much more focused and technical. Are they well-oiled, in fighting trim, and up to efficient employment in battle, or do they need time to be whipped into shape, supplied with essentials, repaired, or retrained?"[42] This discussion from Betts focuses upon "operational" readiness is comparable to when General Meyer addressed the Subcommittee on the Armed Services.[43]

The concept of a hollow force and the lack of operational readiness above are roughly equivalent. Both Betts and Meyer state the same argument, but use different words. Similarly, T. R. Fehrenbach implies that nations need to train soldiers for all missions. "To fail to prepare soldiers and citizens for limited, bloody ground action, and then to engage in it, is folly verging on the criminal."[44]

Following the end of the Cold War, there was no clear threat to U.S. interests as the U.S. emerged as the global superpower. Since there was no clearly identifiable threat, the aforementioned strategy from the 1997 *Quadrennial Defense Review* attempted to provide flexibility to deter conflict before it began, respond swiftly when threats arose, and finally

---

Fehrenbach provides that General MacArthur considers more troops are necessary than only Task Force Smith, which is why MacArthur realizes "two division force" may be needed. T. R. Fehrenbach, *This Kind of War: A Study in Unpreparedness* (New York: The Macmillan Company, 1963), 89.

[41]Betts, *Military Readiness Concepts, Choices, Consequences*, 25.

[42]Ibid., 26.

[43]Ibid.

[44]Fehrenbach, *This Kind of War,* 656.

influence regions to support mutual interests. Following the end of major combat operations in Iraq, a new threat emerged that U.S. Forces were unprepared to deal with, an insurgency. Leaders temporarily struggled to find ideas how to deal with the emerging threat. Changing threats lead to military unpreparedness throughout the force, until leaders understand the change and apply resources in an approach that enables units to train in order to defeat the evolved threat (no matter how primitive).

Technology

Mr. Charles Bloomer wrote similar concerns in an article, "America's Hollow Military." Bloomer calls into question the national military strategy at the time (2000) and the ability for the military to fight two wars simultaneously.[45] Leaders changed the military strategy to being able to respond to engagements separated by at least 45 days. "Our military is over-extended, under-manned, and inadequately equipped."[46] Similar to Senator McCain's comment, the enemy will have a vote on where, how, and definitely when to fight against our forces. Additionally, Mr. James Caratano in his article, "How to Grade a "Hollow" Military," notes that a bipartisan panel from Congress conducted a review in 2010, of the 2010 *Quadrennial Defense Review* report and "concluded that the armed forces lacked the capacity to meet the responsibilities of protecting the U.S. interests worldwide."[47]

The American Enterprise Institute, Foreign Policy Initiative, and The Heritage Foundation highlighted a different variable in an article released in a joint project, "Defending Defense Warning Hollow Force Ahead! The Effect of Ever More Defense Budget Cuts on U.S. Armed Forces." This article discussed how choices to cut the defense budget would affect the future forces after approximately 10 years of combat in both Afghanistan and Iraq. The article

---

[45]Bloomer, "America's hollow army."

[46]Ibid.

[47]James Caratano, "How to Grade a "Hollow" Military," Heritage Network, 7 February 2012, http://blog.heritage.org/2012/02/07/how-to-grade-a-hollow-military/. (accessed 22 August 2012).

addresses the idea, that the "proposed budget cuts represent a small part of future military spending," when in fact, prior to the most recent proposal of $400 billion in cuts, during 2009, "$330 billion was cut from the Pentagon's budget."[48] An additional "$78 billion was sliced from the Pentagon's budget" in 2010.[49]

During the Clinton Presidency, a hiatus or "procurement holiday" of military modernization took place adding to the increased delay in modernization. "Today America's military flies the same basic planes (e.g., F-15, F-16 and F/A-18 fighters; B-52, B-1 and B-2 bombers and a variety of support aircraft) . . . that it did at the end of the Cold War."[50] These, procurement holidays, allow other countries to draw nearer to the same quality of technology as the U.S. thus reducing our superiority on a battlefield.

Mr. James Caratano recently wrote an article, "How to Grade a "Hollow" Military" for the *Heritage Network*. He explains that "warnings about the potential for another "hollow force" arose in 2006" because most of the spending went to current operations in Afghanistan and Iraq and the military equipment being used were being seriously degraded.[51] "Many 'core' military activities–including buying new ships, planes, and vehicles–have been under-funded for decades."[52] He further explained the "warning" in 2006, "was that if we didn't invest to rebuild the military after combat operations in Iraq and Afghanistan ended, the force would "go hollow again." That concern was echoed by the bipartisan panel chartered by Congress in a 2010 review

---

[48]American Enterprise Institute, Foreign Policy Initiative, and The Heritage Foundation, "Defending Defense Warning Hollow Force Ahead! The Effect of Ever More Defense Budget Cuts on U.S. Armed Forces."

[49]Ibid.

[50]Ibid.

[51]Caratano, "How to Grade a "Hollow" Military."

[52]Ibid.

of the Pentagon's *Quadrennial Defense Review* report. The panel concluded that the armed forces lacked the capacity to meet the responsibilities of protecting U.S. interests worldwide."[53]

The Congressional Research Service published an article; "A Historical Perspective on 'Hollow Forces,'" which supports the view that the hollow force following Vietnam was the lack of funding to replace outdated equipment. "The generation of weapons employed during the Vietnam War largely reflected technology developed in the 1950s that was widely seen as obsolete by the end of the war."[54] Although the military consistently uses aging technology, thus far, the U.S. technology remains superior over other countries' technology. What would happen if those countries, who oppose the U.S., gained equal to or greater technological weapons? On the other hand, as simply demonstrated during Operation Iraqi Freedom, the enemy develops weapons such as the improvised explosive devices, or explosively formed penetrators detonated by remote control devices, or by passive systems such as pressure plates. These devices lead Army Specialist Thomas Wilson to ask then Secretary of Defense, Donald Rumsfeld, why units did not have a better-armored vehicle and bulletproof glass. To which Secretary of Defense Rumsfeld responded, "You go to war with the Army you have, not the Army you might want or wish to have at a later time."[55]

Budget priorities within the Department of Defense also may have caused a hollow force following the Vietnam War. "When the defense budget did start to rise slowly between 1976 and 1981, Department of Defense emphasized the procurement of new weapons systems. In the eyes of some critics, the decisions to emphasize modernization over readiness was an error in

---

[53]Ibid.

[54]Daggett and Feickert, *A Historical Perspective on "Hollow Forces."*

[55]Eric Schmitt, "Troops Queries Leave Rumsfeld on the Defensive," *New York Times*, 9 December 2004, http://www.nytimes.com/2004/12/09/international/middleeast/09rumsfeld.html (accessed 22 August 2012).

judgment that left existing units unable to operate."[56] The Congressional Budget Office, similar to Mr. Betts, believes the decisions by existing leadership may have caused part of the hollow Army.

In an article, "Cries of 'Hollow Military' Stifle Rational Debate on Future Spending," Ms. Sandra I. Erwin discusses points of view from leaders who have been through budget cuts in the past like Marine Corps Major General Richard Mills. Mills states, "I've gone through this a couple of times in my career. We continue to function very well." I am not "overly concerned. I say that from experience. I can remember times when it was tough to get fuel for vehicles to go to the field to train, so you walked; when it was tough to get ammunition to shoot for training, but you made do."[57] Additionally, then Army Chief of Staff General Martin Dempsey "told a recent gathering of defense contractors that he expects some budget pains, but he is still certain that the Army will have proper resources to be dominant in the future."[58] Ms. Erwin comments from an article written in the *Washington Post*, "A build-down would not make the military weaker, but leaner and more efficient."[59]

Lack of Numbers

In a 1994 article, "Hollow Forces?: Current Issues of U.S. Military Readiness and Effectiveness," Mr. William W. Kaufman discussed how the variables of military readiness and effectiveness are based upon two factors: "whether the Clinton administration's military forces

---

[56]Congressional Budget Office, "Trends in Selected Indicators of Military Readiness, 1980 Through 1993," 3-4.

[57]Sandra I. Erwin, "Cries of 'Hollow Military' Stifle Rational Debate on Future Spending," *National Defense*, June 2011, http://www.nationaldefensemagazine.org/archive/2011/June/Pages/Criesof%E2%80%98HollowMilitary%E2%80%99StifleRationalDebateonFutureSpending.aspx (accessed 22 August 2012).

[58]Ibid.

[59]Ibid.

are adequate to implement its strategic concept and the size of the forces."[60] This argument shows the mismatch between mission and capability. He argues that the Clinton Administration's strategy and the previous President Bush's strategy "are identical: both assume two virtually simultaneous wars, one starting in the Middle East, to be followed shortly by another on the Korean peninsula, and both require that U.S. and any allied forces effectively demolish opposing military capabilities."[61]

Mr. Kaufman talked about the second variable, size of force.[62] He illustrated the "Bottom-Up Review" conducted by the Clinton Administration. He states, "How could it be that in 1992 the Defense Department said it needed 15 active-duty divisions (12 Army and 3 Marine Corps) as well as 26 Air Force fighter wings (15 active and 11 reserve) when only a year or so later the same department said it required only 13 active-duty divisions (10 Army and 3 Marine Corps) along with 20 Air Force fighter wings (13 active and 7 reserve) for the same planning contingencies and expected outcomes?"[63] Due to a combination of the various service capabilities, Mr. Kaufman argues that a smaller force is capable of meeting contingencies planned based upon strategic missions. "To put the matter another way, smaller U.S. forces on the ground, but larger Air Force tactical fighters than are programmed by the Bottom-Up Review, combined with fewer carrier battle groups, would achieve virtually the same results as the Base or Bottom-Up Review Forces."[64]

Thus far, the literature regarding hollow forces identifies a lack of resources (personnel, operational tempo, readiness, technology, and lack of numbers) as the causes that leads to a

---

[60]William W. Kaufmann, "Hollow Forces? Current Issues of U.S. Military Readiness and Effectiveness," *Brookings Review* (December 1994): 24-29, http://www.unz.org/Pub/ BrookingsRev-1994q4-00024 (accessed 22 August 2012).

[61]Ibid.

[62]Ibid.

[63]Ibid.

[64]Ibid.

hollow force. When the mission exceeds the capabilities of the unit due to inadequate technology, a hollow force exists. Mr. Caratano, in his article, "How to Grade a "Hollow" Military" for the *Heritage Network*, described how money was being spent on the wars in Afghanistan and Iraq and not on the investment of the military. Additionally, he cites how a Congressional panel agreed, following a review of the 2010 *Quadrennial Defense Review*. An article by the Congressional Research Service, "A Historical Perspective on 'Hollow Forces,'" cited how the forces, which fought in Vietnam, used technology from the 1950s. T. R. Fehrenbach in his book, *This Kind of War: A Study in Unpreparedness*, also discussed the lack of technology which hindered Task Force Smith during the Korean War. He stated, "The American Army had developed improved 3.5-inch rocket launchers, which would penetrate the T-34" during the Korean War.[65]

Besides evidence that a hollow force exists due to a lack of the latest technology, the literature above provides intermediate variables as to what leads to a hollow force. Given the superiority of our technology over our adversaries, how does one become a hollow force? Are there any other potential causes of a hollow force that are not prevalent in the current literature? What is a hollow force? These are questions postured to be answered by this document.

Strategic Choices

However, Dr. Richard Betts introduced a different representation of hollow forces.[66] More specifically, in his book, *Military Readiness: Concepts, Choices, Consequences*, he discusses how choices to save money cause military readiness to sink. He writes, "First, military readiness is important: sometimes, as in 1950 and 1990, it is more important than any other public policy matter. The problem is that readiness is only called upon intermittently, indeed rarely, so

---

[65]Fehrenbach, *This Kind of War: A Study in Unpreparedness*, 102.

[66]Although Dr. Betts does not state anything about "hollow forces," however, the root problem of "hollow forces" is not being prepared for their assigned mission, thus military readiness must be discussed.

paying for it over long periods of peacetime can be wasteful."[67] Betts focuses on military readiness rather than hollow forces. For example, "The Clinton administration even raised the priority of the issue by creating an unprecedented high-level overseer, a new undersecretary of defense for personnel and readiness."[68]

The evolution of decisions upon military forces can be found in a monograph by Dr. Richard Meinhart. In Meinhart's monograph, "Strategic Planning by the Chairmen, Joint Chiefs of Staff, 1990 to 2005," he illustrates that during General Shalikashvili's tenure as the Chairman of the Joint Chiefs, he "added long-term direction by publishing the Chairman's first vision and expanded resource advice by adding an analytical assessment process and another resource product" to the strategic planning system.[69] The expansion of this concept providing advice to civilian leaders spawned from the Goldwater-Nichols Department of Defense Reorganization Act of 1986.[70] Surprisingly, "the Chairman has no control over any significant defense resources (Secretary of Defense and Services control resource) or direct control of operational military forces (Combatant Commanders control operational forces)."[71] Additionally one of "the major challenges the Chairmen faced in the 1990s are characterized by the following: global competition and regional instability; increased military operations across the spectrum of conflict; slowly declining financial and personnel resources; rising maintenance and infrastructure costs;

---

[67]Betts, *Military Readiness: Concepts, Choices, Consequences*, 23.

[68]According to Dr. Betts, "The perceived urgency was reflected in additional initiatives: A high-level Senior Readiness Oversight Council, a Readiness Task Force of eight retired generals and admirals under the Defense Science Board, and a midlevel Readiness Working Group." Department of Defense, "Report on the Bottom Up Review," in *Military Readiness: Concepts, Choices, Consequences,* ed. Richard K. Betts, (Washington, DC: The Brookings Institution, 1995), 3.

[69]The process to advise the civilian leaders began as a result of General Shalikashvili's implementation of the *Chairman's Program Recommendation.* Richard Meinhart, "Strategic Planning by the Chairmen, Joint Chiefs of Staff, 1990 to 2005" (Monograph, Strategic Studies Institute, April 2006), http://www.comw.org/qdr/fulltext/0604meinhart.pdf (accessed 22 August 2012), 2.

[70]Meinhart, "Strategic Planning by the Chairmen, Joint Chiefs of Staff, 1990 to 2005," 2.

[71]Ibid., 4.

Cold-War focused equipment; and a need to infuse new technology."[72] Furthermore, "The Chairman formally influences his civilian leaders and those with whom he coordinates through this strategic planning system."[73] The decrease in resources stem from decisions made by the civilian leadership.

In addition, according to Secretary of Defense Robert Gates in the 2010 *Quadrennial Defense Review*, "the Department of Defense balances resources and risk."[74] In order to balance resources the "Secretary took action to direct resources away from lower-priority programs and activities so that more pressing needs could be addressed, both within that budget and in the years that follow it. Those decisions included ending production of the F-22 fighter, restructuring the procurement of the DDG-1000 destroyer and the Future Combat Systems programs, deferring production of new maritime prepositioning ships, and stretching out procurement of a new class of aircraft carrier. The Air Force is substantially reducing its fleet of older fourth-generation fighter aircraft."[75] Through these decisions, the lack of resourcing the latest fielded technology may cause a hollow force within 10 years. The mitigation proposed is "to work with our allies and partners to effectively use limited resources by generating efficiencies and synergies from each other's portfolios of military capabilities."[76]

As a result, from reducing resources, the U.S. hopes to rely on its allies and partners to provide coverage in the gaps within capability and resources. Now risk comes into focus, as the U.S. cannot prescribe terms as she did in the past. "As described earlier, defense strategy requires making choices: accepting and managing risk is thus inherent in everything the Department

---

[72]Ibid.

[73]Ibid.

[74]U.S. Department of Defense, *Quadrennial Defense Review Report* (Washington, DC, February 2010), http://www.defense.gov/qdr/qdr%20as%20of%2029jan10%201600.PDF (accessed 22 August 2012), v.

[75]Ibid., xi.

[76]Ibid., 63.

20

does."[77] Gates lists as an issue "that poses risk to operational missions in the near term include providing sufficient enabling capabilities."[78] Due to decisions to reduce the latest technology, civilian leaders accept the operational risk creating hollow forces. Additionally, he states "these efforts to reduce stress on enablers across the FYDP [Future Years Defense Program], this risk could worsen over time given the projected demands in the future security environment."[79] Institutional risk is also associated with the readiness of forces. Institutional risk is the "shortcomings in the acquisition process put the Department at risk of being unable to deliver the capabilities it needs, when it needs them, and at acceptable costs, and these potential failures in turn threaten the successful execution of military operations."[80] Institutional risk demonstrates when the military require additional technologies in order to complete a mission, the acquisition of those resources may not be available within the time required, which creates a hollow force. Finally, during a period of decreased resources and the acceptance of the risks previously exposed, Admiral Mullen, in an attempt to "balance global strategic risk also requires improving our capabilities to operate in cyberspace" potentially stretching finite resources.[81]

A hollow force exists when the force is unprepared for or incapable of performing its assigned missions. According to Mr. Betts, "Unreadiness occurs when the country finds itself going to war with forces unequal to the task and unable to fight as quickly or effectively as they should, not because their potential is inadequate, but because the decisions necessary to *convert* war potential into available and effective forces were not made soon enough."[82] The potential reasons for this occurrence are when the mission exceeds the capabilities or resources of the unit,

---

[77]Ibid., 89.

[78]Ibid., 90.

[79]Ibid., 91.

[80]Ibid., 93.

[81]M. G. Mullen, "CJCS Guidance 2011," http://www.jcs.mil/content/files/2011-01/011011165132_CJCS_Annual_Guidance_2011.pdf (accessed 22 August 2012), 6.

[82]Betts, *Military Readiness: Concepts, Choices, Consequences*, 28.

21

due to inadequate technology; when the force structure of the unit is inadequate, or, when the force structure and technology is adequate, but the unit lacks the training to complete the type of missions assigned.[83]

Throughout the evolution of warfare, forces changed structures to adapt to emerging technology and different tactics used by enemies. Today, leaders change structure in order to maximize the technological capabilities within a unit structure to ensure the unit has enough capability in order to accomplish the mission assigned.

Lastly, a hollow force arises when the force has not trained or prepared for the mission assigned. This type of hollow force, Betts refers to as the lack of operational readiness and additionally can occur when the mission changes to one operation, for example, from major combat operations to a different mission as counterinsurgency, for which the force has not trained or prepared. This is when a leader assigns a mission such as combined arms maneuver to a force to complete, but the situation required a different mission altogether, for instance wide area security, a change of mission. This phenomenon occurs when the understood environment by leaders changes, resulting in a change of mission by a leader, in order to solve the problem. Adding additional resources to a unit trying to use the wrong approach to the problem, will only waste resources and time.

In summary, the literature review mentions several causes of a hollow force: when a unit lacks the technology to complete an assigned mission; when units lack training to complete the assigned mission; and how the structure (mass) of the force size does not equal the required capability of the assigned mission (see figure 1).[84] According to Michael O'Hanlon, "readiness for assigned missions is only one concern that strategists and policymakers must emphasize. Being ready for a war or other important mission that does not happen is no great solace if a

---

[83]Fehrenbach, *This Kind of War: A Study in Unpreparedness*, 656.

[84]T. R. Fehrenbach and Richard Betts discuss these causes which lead to a "hollow force" or military unreadiness.

country's armed forces prove unready for what they are ultimately asked to do."[85] Other theories

presented within the literature review illustrate possible links to hollow forces, however not the

root cause which, when identified, leaders can prevent the occurrence of hollow forces before

they begin. Additionally, a unit reporting high on readiness could be a hollow force because the

force might be inadequate to complete the mission assigned, either due to the mission exceeding

the units technological capabilities, the structure of the unit is not correct for the mission, or when

the unit is unprepared to conduct the mission assigned. The author will analyze the characteristics

within table 1 with the case studies.

Figure 1. The making of a Hollow Force

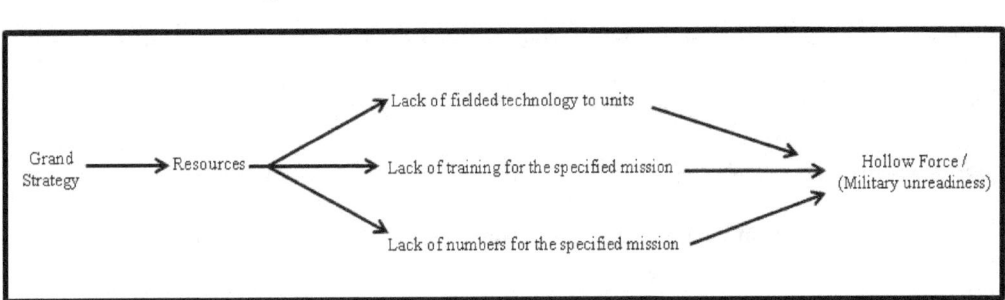

Source: Created by author.

Definitions

Although Mr. Richard Betts and General Meyer state the same idea using different words

(military readiness and hollow forces),the difficulty when dealing with the literature above is that

no two authors have agreed upon a shared characterization of hollow forces or of military

readiness. According to the Congressional Budget Office in the article, "Trends in Selected

Indicators of Military Readiness, 1980 Through 1993," "soon after his [General Meyer's]

testimony, the term hollow force was being widely used to characterize not only the shortages of

---

[85]Michael E. O'Hanlon, *The Science of War* (Princeton, NJ: Princeton University Press, 2009), 31.

experienced personnel but also the shortages of training, weapons, and equipment that undermined military readiness during the mid and late 1970s."[86] Below are the definitions within this study:

Combat Readiness. Synonymous with operational readiness, with respect to missions or functions performed in combat.[87]

Conflict. A time when U.S. Forces use military force against an opponent.

Effectiveness. Mass x Combat Efficiency.

Efficiency. Degree of realized potential of existing force.

Hollow Force. 1) Units that do not have latest technology/equipment to complete their assigned mission. 2) Units that do not have the correct force structure (mass) to complete their assigned mission.[88] 3) Units which lack training on the assigned mission. 4) Units that have inadequate manning and unable to complete their assigned mission.[89]

Mass. Potential capability in existing force (number of organized units).

Mission. In common usage, especially when applied to lower military units, a duty assigned to an individual or unit; a task.[90]

Net Military Readiness. Speed x Effectiveness.[91]

---

[86]Congressional Budget Office, "Trends in Selected Indicators of Military Readiness, 1980 Through 1993," 2.

[87]Joint Chiefs of Staff, Joint Publication 1-02, *Department of Defense Dictionary of Military and Associated Terms* (Washington, DC: Government Printing Office, 8 November 2010 (as amended through 15 January 2012)), 57.

[88]Charles Boomer, in his article "America's Hollow Military," uses elements of definitions (1), (2) and (4). He cites the drawdown of manning only reduces personnel, not force structure or structural readiness according to Richard Betts. Boomer also discusses concerns of how a lighter force may not be able to fight a "heavy" war containing tanks.

[89]Definition (4) is common among military leaders who served following the Vietnam War and does not expand on any additional factors added as a possibility leading to "hollow forces." Retired Army Colonel William Darryl Henderson in his book, *The Hollow Army: How the U.S. Army is Oversold and Undermanned* uses this definition.

[90]Joint Chiefs of Staff, Joint Publication 1-02, 215.

Operational Readiness. Speed x Efficiency.[92] The capability of a unit or formation, ship, weapon system, or equipment to perform the missions or functions for which it is organized or designed. Also called OR, See also combat readiness.[93]

Personnel Readiness. "Personnel available and qualified to perform assigned missions or functions."[94]

Speed. Time in which unit is deployed into combat.

Structural Readiness. Speed x Mass.[95]

Methodology

The purpose of this study is to explore the potential causes that lead to a hollow force following prolonged combat operations. The author hypothesized, following research of a hollow force, that strategic choices from grand strategy cause a decline in resources, which is likely to lead to a hollow force in the U.S. Army in the next decade after prolonged combat operations. Employing the case study method, the author will analyze the independent variables of technology, structure (size/composition), and threat against potential reasons congruent with hollow forces.

According to Stephen Van Evera in his book, *Guide to Methods for Students of Political Science*, "case studies can be best if we want to infer or test explanatory hypotheses or if cases have been unevenly recorded–a few are recorded in great detail, many in scant detail."[96] The

---

[91] The definitions from Net military readiness and below to Structural readiness come from Dr. Richard Betts book, *Military Readiness: Concepts, Choices, Consequences* from Table 2-1, page 40.

[92] Ibid.

[93] Joint Chiefs of Staff, Joint Publication 1-02, 247.

[94] Ibid.

[95] The definition of operational and structural readiness, which also comes from Dr. Richard Betts book, *Military Readiness: Concepts, Choices, Consequences* from Table 2-1 page 40, equal the definition of "hollow forces used in the case studies.

[96] Stephen Van Evera, *Guide to Methods for Students of Political Science* (Ithaca, NY: Cornell University Press, 1997), 55.

author will observe these variables using case studies in order to determine congruence or incongruence for potential causality for a hollow U.S. Army. In 1980, only three decades ago, General Meyer first used the term hollow force, when he referred to the forces following the Vietnam War. Scholars neglect the possible hollow forces during periods preceding the Vietnam War.

In order to test the author's theory, the criteria used to select the case studies represent extreme low values on the dependent variable of military readiness. The cases identified have only one or two occasions within the 10 year period where the U.S. participates in a major conflict. Additionally, these case studies "are well matched for controlled cross-case comparisons" because the case following the Vietnam War provides a basis for comparison.[97]

The author will illustrate by using the method of similarities according to the model with the cases selected. The original, and likely only cited case of a hollow force, is the period following the Vietnam War. Most of the literature references this period and agree when referring to a hollow force. However, the characteristics of this period illustrate only one independent variable; force (manning) that caused the hollow force. The author provides several independent variables because no agreed definition of hollow forces exists. The cause of one type of hollow force may differ from other types; however, all result from resource shortfalls.

Although General Meyer recently originated the term hollow force, the range of case studies runs throughout American battles, not just following the Vietnam War. This study will examine the following case studies: the period following World War II (Korean War), the period following the Gulf War (Desert Storm) and lastly, the period following 11 September 2001 (the beginning of Operation Enduring Freedom). Each case study covers a period following prolonged conflict.

---

[97]Ibid., 84.

Variables

Within the literature, authors cited many different variables that cause a hollow force: the decline of manning, military readiness, pay and benefits, technology, budget decreases, budget priorities, operational tempo, the threat, too many national interests, and even decisions from leaders. Authors referenced many and different variables that lead to a possibility of a lack of readiness or unreadiness as Mr. James Kitfield purported.[98] According to Mr. Stephen Van Evera, intervening variables are "variables framing intervening phenomenon included in a causal theory's explanation. Intervening phenomena are caused by the independent variable and cause the dependent variable."[99] While these variables contribute to creating a hollow force, most authors are unaware of the independent variables, which actually cause a hollow force.

According to Mr. Van Evera, the dependent variable "caused the causal theory or hypothesis."[100] Simply stated, without the presence of independent variables, the dependent variable will not occur. Individuals who understand this concept possess the ability to change the potential outcomes pending the correct identification of the independent variables, which cause the dependent variable.

As mentioned above, the times in which a force may be hollow are the following: when units have inadequate technology/equipment to complete their assigned mission; when units that do not have the correct force structure (size/composition) to complete their assigned mission;[101] when units lack training on the assigned mission; and when units that have inadequate manning

---

[98]Kitfield, "The Hollow Force Myth."

[99]Van Evera, *Guide to Methods for Students of Political Science*, 11.

[100]Ibid.

[101]Charles Boomer, in his article "America's Hollow Military," uses elements of both definitions (1), (2) and (4). He cites the drawdown of manning only reduces personnel, not force structure. He also discusses concerns of how a lighter force may not be able to fight a "heavy" war containing tanks.

and are unable to complete their assigned mission.[102] During these times the force is incapable of completing its assigned mission and is hollow.

Although Meyer created the term hollow force in 1980, the case studies below illustrate that hollow forces presented themselves during other times, not just following the Vietnam War. The purpose of demonstrating when hollow forces existed other than after the Vietnam War is to warn leaders that hollow forces exist more frequently, but at any level, leaders who identify probable hollowness have the opportunity to create change to avoid creating hollow forces.

The author will use the following study variables as independent variables in this study: technology, training, and numbers. The dependent variable will be the mission of the force.

Case Studies

General Joseph F. Dunford Jr. recently testified before a Congressional Subcommittee:

> And then I would just say the last thing that keeps me awake at night is all of us came in the military in the late 1970s, and I was a platoon commander in the post-Vietnam days. And I know what a hollow force is because I was a platoon commander in a hollow force. And I will tell you that the number one thing that keeps me awake at night is begin a part of anything that would cause the U.S. Marine Corps to look like it did in the 1970s as opposed to what it looks like in 2012. That is really what keeps me awake at night.[103]

The case studies illustrated within this study demonstrate the different examples of a hollow force and the possible causes. The case studies examined are the period during the Korean War, the periods following the Vietnam War and the Gulf War, and the present day. This study will determine if a hollow force existed during these periods. The case studies will evaluate, using

---

[102]Definition (4) is common among military leaders who served following the Vietnam War and does not expand on any additional factors added as a possibility leading to "hollow forces." Retired Army Colonel William Darryl Henderson in his book, *The Hollow Army: How the U.S. Army is Oversold and Undermanned* uses this definition.

[103]During testimony provided by General Joseph F. Dunford, Jr., USMC, Assistant Commandant, U.S. Marine Corps. Hearing to Receive Testimony on the Current Readiness of U.S. Forces in Review of the Defense Authorization Request for Fiscal Year 2013 and the Future Years Defense Program, http://armed-services.senate.gov/Transcripts/2012/ 05%20May/12-37%20-%205-10-12.pdf (accessed 22 August 2012), 10.

table 1, whether the lack of the latest technology, lack of specified training for the mission, or insufficient numbers led to a hollow force.

Korean War

The Korean War began almost 30 years before the origination of the term hollow forces by General Meyers. However, a historical case such as the Korean War reveals that hollow forces existed. One must examine the background surrounding the Korean War case study and then connect relationships between the causes of a hollow force during that period. Many may argue that American forces serving in Korea succeeded in accomplishing their assigned missions. This author also agrees; however, leaders' decisions following World War II assisted in constructing hollow forces during the Korean War. The following case study will analyze the surroundings and possible causes of a hollow force in the years following World War II.

Following the attack by Japan at Pearl Harbor in 1941, the United States finally entered World War II. However, the armed forces required troops and equipment, and the American people and industry answered that call with both people and equipment. The United States, combined with other Allied powers, fought a two-front war, Nazi Germany in Europe and Imperial Japan in the Pacific. After the Germans and the Japanese surrendered officially, World War II ended and a transition for the armed forces began.

The United States' forces occupied Germany while performing a range of civil affairs or "law and order" duties within Germany.[104] At the beginning of the occupation, President Eisenhower "had sixty-one U.S. divisions, 1,622,000 men, in Germany, and a total force in Europe numbering 3,077,000."[105] The mission assigned in war-torn Germany was difficult. "Leaders and troops were called upon to deal with a series of complex challenges in political,

---

[104]Earl F. Ziemke, *Army Historical Series: The U.S. Army in the Occupation of Germany1944-1946*, http://www.history.army.mil/books/wwii/Occ-GY/ch18.htm#b1 (accessed 22 August 2012), 320.

[105]Ibid.

financial, social, and cultural affairs, tasks beyond the traditional roles of soldiers."[106] Similarly,

forces conducted law enforcement patrols in occupied Japan, since Japan's surrender on

2 September 1945

The United States no longer required the large force structure required to fight the two-

front war any longer, and only maintained enough forces for the current foreseen missions within

occupied Germany and Japan. "Active manpower in uniform declined from about 12 million at

the end of the war to about 1 ½ million five years later."[107] Therefore, the United States

government conducted a reduction in forces from both theaters of war in order to release

economic pressures and to return the United States to a sense of normalcy. From this decision,

one can conclude when the hollow force spawned. While reducing the number of personnel, mass

also declines creating a potential for decreased unit numbers and a decrease in structural

readiness.[108] "The U.S. Army had a nominal total of ten divisions in the active force, but these

were almost all under strength and were kept on the books as combat units only by cutting the

support elements vital for moving and sustaining them."[109]

United States leaders did not anticipate the North Korean invasion of South Korea on

25 June 1950. They were unable to expand the force structure in a rapid manner to counterattack

the North Korean Army to cease the potential spread of communism. Overall net military

readiness decreases due to the inability to move forces rapidly into combat.[110] Leaders accepted

the risk of defeat in South Korea when they decided not to move forces assigned to missions in

---

[106]Ibid.

[107]Betts, *Military Readiness: Concepts, Choices, Consequences*, 16.

[108]Richard Betts, *Military Readiness: Concepts, Choices, Consequences*, "Structural readiness concerns *mass*; it is about how soon a force of the size necessary to deal with the enemy can be available. Structural readiness refers to the number of personnel under arms with at least basic training, the number of formations in which they are organized the quantity and quality of their weapons, and the distribution of combat assets among land, sea, and air power," 41.

[109]Betts, *Military Readiness: Concepts, Choices, Consequences*, 17.

[110]Ibid., 40.

Europe due to the importance of "the orderly containment of communism. Americans had learned much . . . for both sides understood the stakes in Europe were too vital to risk less than all-out effort, if force were used."[111] "Germany and Japan had to be occupied."[112] The North Korean Army and spread of communism were the hazards United States leadership faced. Leadership used forces within Japan to mitigate the North Korean threat. Increased time was the opportunity desired by the leadership, in which planners created a more thoughtful plan of action. Because of the strategic decision a mismatch between the force from Japan and the mission occurred. Additionally, the forces were deficient in training and lacked the structural readiness and the operational readiness to perform the assigned mission.

Likewise, another factor, which caused the forces from Japan assigned to the mission to South Korea to be hollow, was training. Task Force Smith had little time to train for combined arms maneuver operations prior to heading to South Korea. Upon receipt of the mission, units normally trained in the tasks they most likely would perform during the mission. Leaders assigned Task Force Smith a constable mission in Japan, but when the North Korean Army attacked into South Korea, leaders changed the focus to a combined arms maneuver mission to execute rapidly. Although "training for combat replaced occupation as their primary mission a year before the North Korean attack, there were not enough training ranges available in the country (of Japan) for practicing fire and maneuver."[113] "And the training wasn't bad. There were no real training areas in crowded Nippon, so there wasn't much even General Walker of Eighth Army could do about that, though he made noises."[114] Unprepared, the Task Force executed the assigned mission on the Korean peninsula; however, Task Force Smith was a hollow force because it could not complete the assigned mission regardless of the operational readiness. Task

---

[111] The sides Fehrenbach refers to are the United States and the Soviet Union. Fehrenbach, *This Kind of War: A Study in Unpreparedness*, 47.

[112] Betts, *Military Readiness: Concepts, Choices, Consequences*, 15.

[113] Ibid., 17.

[114] Fehrenbach, *This Kind of War: A Study in Unpreparedness*, 100.

Force Smith had limited additional training (if any) following the receipt of mission, due to the lack of time prior to the execution of the mission.[115] "Armor Units formed, but personnel were dragged out of units all over the Eighth Army and from Fort Hood in Texas, yet many of those in the new unit were not Armor specialists. A battalion landed in Korea on 7 August and went straight into combat–a complete bunch of strangers with no training."[116] "Task Force Smith had neither arms nor training."[117]

Additionally, the lack of existing technology created a hollow force as well. "Task Force Smith had to borrow equipment from other battalions, and units that followed were missing such basic items as mortar components and recoilless rifles."[118] Task Force Smith had "two 75mm recoilless rifles, two 4.2-inch mortars, six 2.36 inch rocket launchers, and four 60mm mortars."[119] Also, the only armor available at the time "were war-weary M-24 Chaffee light tanks, which were no match for the North Koreans' T-34s."[120] T. R. Fehrenbach provides a similar account of structural readiness:

> [A]nd nine separate regimental combat teams, all of which, except the one in Europe, were at 70 percent strength. Each regiment had, instead of its normal three battalions, only two, and each artillery battalion had not its proper three firing batteries, but two.
>
> No division had its proper wartime quota of weapons and equipment, and each had only light M024 tanks. What equipment each division had was World War II worn, and old.[121]

An example of the lack of technology occurred when "Lieutenant Ollie Connor, watching, grabbed a bazooka and ran down to the ditch alongside the road. Steadying the

---

[115]Task Force Smith reported "at a little past eight on the morning of 1 July 1950 . . . at Itazuke Air Base." This was only six days following the beginning of the war.

[116]Betts, *Military Readiness: Concepts, Choices, Consequences*, 18-19.

[117]Fehrenbach, *This Kind of War: A Study in Unpreparedness*, 103.

[118]Betts, *Military Readiness: Concepts, Choices, Consequences*, 18.

[119]Fehrenbach, *This Kind of War: A Study in Unpreparedness*, 98.

[120]Betts, *Military Readiness: Concepts, Choices, Consequences*, 18.

[121]Fehrenbach, *This Kind of War: A Study in Unpreparedness*, 91.

2.36-inch rocket launcher on the nearest tank, only fifteen yards away, Conner let fly. The small shaped charge burned out against the thick Russian armor without penetrating."[122]

Besides the factors above, a lack of coordination or shared doctrine played a part in the lack of readiness. According to Richard Betts, when units got to Korea, they "had no means of coordinating with South Korean forces, and command and control arrangements among themselves were completely inadequate. Air-ground operations, the one special advantage available to U.S. forces, were also poorly coordinated."[123]

A common theme surrounding hollow forces is risk. The reason risk is prevalent within our forces is because forces, including hollow forces, are unable to train for every anticipated mission. Today, leaders accept risk during training by focusing on the toughest mission, combined arms maneuver, not every contingency that may occur. Leaders make the assumption, if forces are capable of performing combined arms maneuver against another force, the unit will be able to perform a mission of lesser difficulty satisfactorily, in order to gain time for leaders to apply a correct force structure or resources to solve the problem favorable to the interests of the United States.

In summary, the post-World War II period proved difficult for American Forces specifically for those fighting the Korean War. After the completion of World War II, the American forces became constables and civil leaders throughout Europe and Japan. Structural readiness decreased due to the demobilization of force. Operational readiness decreased due to the inability to train. Additionally, the lack of shared doctrine caused a decrease in readiness across the combined American and South Korean forces. When leadership tasked Task Force Smith with the mission to quickly stop and defeat North Korean forces, the mission proved overreaching and the mass (size) of the force was too small to complete the mission.

---

[122]Ibid., 101.

[123]Betts, *Military Readiness: Concepts, Choices, Consequences*, 17.

After Vietnam

Following the Vietnam War, the United States forces were in shambles. The war, among other highly publicized actions, damaged the reputation of the armed forces and the confidence of the American people. Congress passed the law ending the draft and creating the All-Volunteer Force in 1973.[124] Moreover, personnel issues such as pay, discipline, and recruitment reverberated throughout the forces. "Early years of the all-volunteer force witnessed a significant drop in education levels and test scores among recruits, widespread scandals, and increases in bad discharges and peacetime desertions. Salaries did not keep up with high levels of inflation during the remainder of the 1970s and fell progressively further and further behind the cost of living."[125] Additionally, "in 1979, Army commissaries reportedly accepted almost $10 million in food stamps from service members."[126]

General Dunford, as a witness before Congress, purported the hollowness of the forces following the Vietnam War as did General Meyer during his testimony before Congress referencing units that were zeroed out and effectively lacking the full capability to accomplish a mission assigned. Generals continue to reference hollow forces when discussing readiness with members of Congress today.

Michael E. O'Hanlon states in *The Science of War*, about the forces during the 1970s, "A substantial force structure existed, but it did not hold up very well when called upon to perform."[127] Although the transition to an All-Volunteer Force proved difficult, the forces lacked training. On 4 November 1979, captors held 52 American hostages in Tehran, Iran. President Carter's National Security Advisor, Zbignew Brzezinski, had "telephoned Secretary of Defense

---

[124]RAND Corporation, "The Evolution of the All-Volunteer Force" (Research Brief, 2006), http://www.rand.org/pubs/research_briefs/RB9195/index1.html (accessed 22 August 2012).

[125]Daggett and Feickert, *A Historical Perspective on "Hollow Forces,"* 3.

[126]Ibid., 5.

[127]O'Hanlon, *The Science of War*, 31.

34

Harold Brown and instructed him to have the Joint Chiefs of Staff develop a plan for a rescue mission" on Nov 6, 1979—two days after the Americans were taken hostage in Tehran."[128] On 24 April 1980 a RH-53 Helicopter "while repositioning during the refueling operation, a helicopter slammed into a C-130, immediately engulfing both aircraft in flames, killing eight crew members and injuring five."[129] This routine movement of a helicopter demonstrated the lack of operational readiness and training of the force, to rescue the hostages.

Additionally, during the mission the equipment malfunctioned as well. The mission began with eight RH-53 Helicopters. These helicopters were outfitted with "mine-sweeping equipment and 2 x 12.7mm Browning heavy machine guns for the purpose of exploding mines in the water."[130] "Two hours into the journey, one of the helicopters' rotor blades malfunctioned."[131] After going through a sand storm, "Another helicopter malfunctioned and opted to return to the Nimitz."[132] Lastly as the helicopters arrived to the refueling point which consisted of a C130 and pathfinders, "One of the helicopters' hydraulic pumps failed on the way to the refueling spot. There was no replacement pump, and there'd have been no time to replace it had there been one."[133] The Navy replaced the RH-53 Helicopters with the MH-53E based upon the CH-53E model released in 1981.[134]

---

[128]Pierre Tristam, "The Failed Rescue of American Hostages in Iran on April 24, 1980," About.com. Middle East Issues, http://middleeast.about.com/od/usmideastpolicy/a/me090413b.htm (accessed 22 August 2012).

[129]Pierre Tristam, "What was Operation Eagle Claw, the Failed Rescue of American Hostages in Iran?," About.com. Middle East Issues, http://middleeast.about.com/od/usmideastpolicy/f/me090413c.htm (accessed 22 August 2012).

[130]Military Factory, "Sikorsky CH-53Sea Lion Heavy-Lift Transport Helicopter," last updated 5 February 2011, http://www.militaryfactory.com/aircraft/detail.asp?aircraft_id=178 (accessed 22 August 2012).

[131]Tristam, "What was Operation Eagle Claw, the Failed Rescue of American Hostages in Iran?"

[132]Ibid. The Nimitz is where the helicopters and crews began the operation.

[133]Ibid.

[134]Military Factory, "Sikorsky CH-53Sea Lion Heavy-Lift Transport Helicopter."

The structural readiness of this operational force to move across "600-mile journey at low altitude, below radar detection, to a refueling stop in the Iranian desert," consisted of eight RH-53 Helicopters.[135] The commanders of the operation determined the minimum number of helicopters required to be six. At the beginning, the force numbers were adequate. Following the technical difficulties with the three RH-53 Helicopters, "The mission was down to five operational helicopters, one short of the minimum commanders had agreed was required to succeed in a hostage rescue."[136] With the reduction of the RH-53 Helicopters, structural readiness declined, which also decreased operational readiness for the rescue mission.[137] Due to unforeseen changes, leaders chose to cancel the mission to free the hostages because of the lack of numbers required.

Another scenario after Vietnam is that of the Grenada, where President Ronald Reagan sent forces to rescue students, who were studying on the island, from the Provisional Revolutionary Government which took control of the island following an uprising. The forces, sent by Reagan were a joint force consisting of Delta, Rangers, Navy Seals and elements from the 82nd Airborne Division.[138]

An example, albeit a tragedy, which demonstrates lack of training and operational readiness in Grenada is when "a Navy A-7 air strike was called in by a Marine ANGLICO (Air, Naval Gunfire Liaison Company) Officer attached to the 82nd. In a tragic accident, he misidentified the target to the Navy jets, and one aircraft strafed a group of 82nd paratroops

---

[135]Tristam, "What was Operation Eagle Claw, the Failed Rescue of American Hostages in Iran?"

[136]Ibid.

[137]Structural readiness equals mass times speed. As the number of RH-53 helicopters decreased below the minimum number required for the operation, the "hollow force" emerged.

[138]M. Albert Mendez and Lee Russell, Illustrated by Paul Hannon, *Granada 1983* (Great Britain: Osprey Publishing Ltd, 1985). General Meyer exempted the 82nd Airborne Division as being hollow in his testimony to Congress. The other units mentioned are those in which Operational Readiness is extremely high and are typically always assigned the most difficult missions to accomplish before active duty forces (like the 82nd Airborne Division) are tasked. Consider a counterfactual of a different unit replacing any of these in Grenada, what would have happened?

setting up a tactical command post amid some former Cuban barracks. The attack wounded 16 soldiers, one of whom later died."[139] Granted, the authors did not provide any extenuating circumstances, however, training and a clear marking system could have avoided this unfortunate incident.[140]

In summary, following Vietnam, a lack of training and operational readiness occurred within the forces during the hostage attempt in Iran as well as in the Grenada mission, which caused the cancellation of the rescue of hostages in Iran and the death of one soldier and 15 others wounded in Grenada. Likewise, the lack of numbers within the force occurred due to the loss of three RH-53 Helicopters causing leaders to cancel the mission.

After the Cold War

Following the end of the Cold War and the collapse of the Soviet Union, the United States found itself as the last superpower. Forces structural readiness and operational readiness levels waned as a result; for there were no potential adversaries with the capability similar to the Soviet Union. The 1990s began with the Gulf War when Iraq, under President Saddam Hussein invaded Kuwait on 2 August 1990. Hussein wanted to forcibly seize the oil resources and land based on historical claims that Kuwait was part of original Iraq and, possibly, to unify the Arabs. King Fahd of Saudi Arabia requested assistance from the United States in ousting Iraq from Kuwait, possibly because Saudi Arabia also felt the potential threat by Hussein to attack and unify Saudi Arabia as well.[141] The United States led a coalition of forces to eradicate Iraqi forces from Kuwait. After a shaping air bombing operation, the coalition conducted a ground attack from Saudi Arabia into both Kuwait and Southern Iraq. In 100 hour ground war, leadership called

---

[139]Mendez, Russell, and Hannon, *Granada 1983*, 33-34.

[140]The author understands this is only one isolated example in Grenada, however, the example demonstrates a theme following Vietnam. Additionally, according to Betts in his book, *Military Readiness: Concepts, Choices, Consequences*, 23. "Getting the answer wrong exacts a price in one currency or the other: either in blood in wartime or in treasure in peacetime."

[141]PBS frontline: Chronology the Gulf War, http://www.pbs.org/wgbh/ pages/frontline/gulf/cron/. (accessed 22 August 2012).

a cease-fire for hostilities. The coalition succeeded attaining its operational goal. Below the study will provide an analysis of the Gulf War forces to determine a potential hollow force.

The coalition force began air attacks on 17 January 1991, and completed the ground war on 2 March 1991.[142] Mr. Betts states in *Military Readiness: Choices, Concepts, Consequences,* "The nearly perfect performance of U.S. forces in operations against Iraq was due in large part to three factors."[143] The factors are the following:

1. <u>Readiness for what: the choice of enemy</u>. Iraq's military power was high in quantity but low in quality. Baghdad had bought a modern military machine . . . while modernizing, remained primitive in several important respects. Training was especially deficient, because of political inhibitions as well as limited resources and education.

2. <u>Readiness for when: time to prepare for combat</u>. The full potential of existing structural readiness was realized, as time and rapidly infused resources were exploited to achieve maximum operational readiness. Between the invasion of Kuwait in August 1990 and the beginning of the air war in January 1991, the American military mobilized, filled out, and deployed units to Saudi Arabia; set up bases, headquarters, logistical networks, communications systems, and supply stockpiles; and trained over, and over, and over again for the attack.

3. <u>Readiness of what: capitalization on the Cold War</u>. The United States fought Iraq with forces developed over the course of four decades of mobilization for war with a superpower, the Soviet Union. The Reagan buildup, which had boosted the regular baseline of Cold War capabilities, had also crested not long before Saddam Hussein struck. Since the Cold War had ended months before the invasion of Kuwait, this meant that "available structural readiness was higher than needed" to fight Iraq.[144]

---

[142]Ibid.

[143]Betts, *Military Readiness: Concepts, Choices, Consequences,* 184.

[144]Ibid., 184-185.

Time allowed the forces' readiness to increase. "Although the readiest of army reserve units were called to service first, 15 percent of those mobilized in the first three months of Desert Shield were rated not deployable (that is, below C-3); during the following two months, more than one-third of army units that were called up were rated not deployable."[145] To resolve logistical readiness issues leaders decided to transfer equipment stores from Europe. "Some readiness problems were eased by violating earlier Cold War plans that allocated the bulk of capabilities to deterring Soviet attack in Europe."[146]

Training was not a factor for the gathered operational forces. Dr. Stephen Bourque in *JAYHAWK! The Seventh Corps in the Persian Gulf War*, states how the U.S. Army went through a transition in training:

> The U.S. Army that arrived in the Gulf in the fall and winter of 1990 was the product of a recent revolution in military training. Before 1975 unit commanders measured training effectiveness by time. How long did the unit remain in the field? How many hours of such and such training did the unit experience? Missing, of course, was any analysis as to the effectiveness of the training. There were no training objectives and standards of performance that indicated how well the unit or soldier actually performed the mission.[147]

Additionally, the equipment of these forces was far superior to Iraq's equipment. "In terms of equipment, it was a vastly more sophisticated force. The standard tank was the M1 Abrams and later M1A1 (improved version) that added combined speed and firepower to a comprehensive and reliable package. A proportion of the mechanized infantry that worked in concert with the heavy armor also used the relatively new Bradley fighting vehicle (M2IFV and M3CFV) with its powerful 25mm chain gun and two TOW (tube launched optically tracked wire-guided) anti-tank missiles."[148] The common soldier carried the basic rifle, "M16A2, a perfected

---

[145]Ibid., 187.

[146]Ibid.

[147]Stephen Bourque, *JAYHAWK! The Seventh Corps in the Persian Gulf War* (Washington, DC: Department of the Army, 2002), 103.

[148]Alistair Finlan, *The Gulf War 1991: Essential Histories* (Great Britain: Osprey Publishing, 2003), 22.

version of an earlier model that had proved susceptible to the dust of south-east Asia and in Vietnam had developed a nasty habit of jamming at critical moments."[149]

The Gulf War poses a historical example of how to conduct war and having time and a little luck on the side of the United States. The case study does not illustrate a hollow force for accidental reasons. The Cold War had only recently ended when Hussein invaded Kuwait. Forces were well trained while preparing for the war with the Soviet Union. Likewise, the force had the latest technology to use. Lastly, the decisions to use a Coalition Force stacked against the mission of expelling the Iraq Forces did not create an unbalance in force numbers.

Present day

Following over 10 years of war in both Afghanistan and Iraq since the destruction of the World Trade Towers on 11 September 2001, the United States decreased the numbers of soldiers and units in Iraq. Additionally, the number of units in Afghanistan will condense at the end of 2014. However, "The United States and North Atlantic Treaty Organization allies affirmed a plan that would leave international forces in a noncombat, supportive role in Afghanistan by the end of 2014." [150] The buildup of forces and restructuring of the 10 active divisions occurred as a response to ease the possible strain on the All-Volunteer Army. In January of 2004 and following the invasion of Iraq, Army Chief of Staff, General Peter Schoomaker "briefed the House Armed Services Committee on plans to restructure the Army's current organization which retains the 10 division headquarters as battle command headquarters. The Army would increase the number of brigades under those divisions from three maneuver brigades to four. That alone would take the service from 30 brigades under the division structure to 40 (plus two armored cavalry regiments

---

[149]Ibid.

[150]Michael Bowman, "Obama Administration Defends Afghanistan Timeline," voanews.com, 27 May 2012, http://www.voanews.com/content/obama_administration_ defends_afghanistan_withdrawal_timeline/1105882.html (accessed 22 August 2012).

and the 173rd Airborne Brigade) by FY 2007."[151] Additionally, the number of active duty soldiers increased from 480,801 in 2001 to 565,463 in 2011.[152] Lastly, military training for these units has mainly encompassed counterinsurgency training versus combined arms maneuvers, used for fighting conventional forces. Therefore, the question, which remains to be answered, is will the U.S. military be hollow again? Decisions by leaders are creating the perfect hollow storm. According to President Obama, those decisions are required because "we must put our fiscal house in order here at home."[153]

In a 2011 article, "Military Already Being Cut, But Obama Makes It Official," by Mackenzie Eaglen, asserts "President Obama on Wednesday announced $400 billion in defense cuts between now and 2023."[154] With this decision from Obama, difficult choices by the Department of Defense must occur. According to Thom Shanker and Elisabeth Bumiller in a *New York Times* article, "In New Strategy, Panetta Plans Even Smaller Army," "The new military strategy is driven by at least $450 billion in Pentagon budget cuts over the next decade."[155] Furthermore, "Defense Secretary Leon E. Panetta has concluded that the Army has to shrink even below current targets, dropping to 490,000 soldiers over the next decade. These reductions in troop levels can occur over the next six years according to the 2012 article "Earlier Drawdowns

---

[151]GlobalSecurity.org, "Brigade Unit of Action," http://www.globalsecurity.org/military/agency/army/bua.htm (accessed 22 August 2012).

[152]Infoplease, "Active Duty Personnel," http://www.infoplease.com/ipa/A0004598.html (accessed 22 August 2012).

[153]U.S. Department of Defense, "Sustaining U.S. Global Leadership: Priorities for 21st Century Defense," Washington, DC: January 2012, http://www.defense.gov/news/Defense_Strategic_Guidance.pdf (accessed 22 August 2012).

[154]Mackenzie Eaglen, "Military Already Being Cut, But Obama Makes It Official," *The Foundry*, 13 April 2011, http://blog.heritage.org/2011/04/13/military-already-being-cut-but-obama-makes-it-official/ (accessed 22 August 2012).

[155]Elisabeth Bumiller and Thom Shanker, "In New Strategy, Panetta Plans Even Smaller Army," *New York Times*, 5 January 2012, http://www.nytimes.com/2012/01/05/us/in-new-strategy-panetta-plans-even-smaller-army.html (accessed 22 August 2012).

Give Idea of What Is to Come," by Mr. Jim Tice. "Six years is the timeline that defense and Army leaders stipulate for the upcoming force reduction."[156]

By the same token to avoid the zeroed out units referred to by General Meyer, the number of Brigade Combat Teams will be reduced.[157] According to the article "Odierno: Brigade Cuts Needed to Reorganize," by Lance Bacon, "The reduction of five more brigade combat teams is necessary to add a third maneuver battalion and an engineer battalion in each brigade, the Army's top officer said Feb. 24."[158] This reduction of Brigade Combat Teams will provide more combat power for each individual Brigade Combat Team and reduce the number of zeroed out units due to the reduction in forces. The decreased amount of Brigade Combat Teams may result in a lack of numbers within the force depending upon the unforeseen missions assigned by civilian leaders.

Military equipment, also becomes a concern for leaders, although their assessments lean toward prudent decisions. According to former Secretary of Defense Robert Gates in the *Quadrennial Defense Review Report*:

> Our assessment of ongoing and potential future military operations identified a significant number of possible shortfalls in the capabilities or capacity of programmed U.S. forces. In some cases, opportunities exist to remedy these shortfalls by investing in new systems or additional force structure. In other cases, no readily available solutions are at hand but greater investments in research and development or concept exploration are warranted. Of course, many of these enhancements will be costly. Some of the tradeoffs that DoD's leaders have identified to enable the rebalancing of U.S. military capabilities are described below. More such tradeoffs could be necessary in the future.[159]

---

[156]Jim Tice, "Earlier Drawdowns Give Idea of What Is to Come," Army Forum, http://www.armytimes.com/news/2012/02/army-earlier-drawdowns-give-idea-whats-to-come-021912w/ (accessed 22 August 2012).

[157]U.S. Congress, House of Representatives, *National Defense Funding Levels for Fiscal Year 1981*, 18.

[158]Lance M. Bacon, "Odierno: Brigade Cuts Needed to Reorganize," *Army Times*, 3 March 2012, http://www.armytimes.com/news/2012/03/army-ray-odierno-says-brigade-combat-team-cuts-needed-reorganize-030312w/. (accessed 22 August 2012).

[159]U.S. Department of Defense, *Quadrennial Defense Review Report*.

However, according to Mr. Owen Graham, "After 10 years of war and major wear and tear on military equipment, the military is in dire shape and needs to be modernized."[160] Coupled with modernizing military equipment, Mackenzie Eaglen, in the article "Military Already Being Cut, But Obama Makes It Official," argues, "Only $100 billion is technically considered "savings" resulting from efficiency initiatives and reforms at the Pentagon. The remaining $300 billion in defense cuts the President would like to emulate resulted from significant cuts through the cancelation or delaying of over 50 major weapons programs. The list of defense cuts includes a combat search and rescue helicopter, the F-22 fifth generation fighter, the Army's future combat systems (primarily a ground vehicle program), the multiple-kill vehicle for missile defense, a bomber for the Air Force, the VH-71 presidential helicopter, a transformational satellite program, and the second airborne laser aircraft."[161]

Lastly, one must consider training of military units. Prior to the invasion of Iraq in March of 2003, units trained for combined arms maneuver operations. However, following the identification of an Iraqi insurgency in 2004 to the present, military forces have trained upon counterinsurgency operations. In an August 2012 article, "Army Adapts to Post-Afghanistan Mission," Matthew Cox illustrates how the Army continues to stray away from lethal combined arms maneuver training. Instead, "Early next year, soldiers from the 1st Infantry Division will shelve their combat experience from the Middle East to become training advisors to African forces. The 2nd Heavy Brigade Combat Team out of Fort Riley, Kansas, will become the Army's first "regionally-aligned" brigade assigned to U.S. Africa command."[162] The author agrees with the concept of regionally aligned units. However, when will the Army allow these units to train

---

[160]Owen Graham, "Armed Forces Face Major Cuts in Budget," posted 21 August 2012, http://www.vindy.com/news/2012/aug/21/armed-forces-face-major-cuts-in-budgets/?newswatch (accessed 22 August 2012).

[161]Eaglen, "Military Already Being Cut, But Obama Makes It Official."

[162]Matthew Cox, "Army Adapts to Post-Afghanistan Mission," 9 August 2012, http://www.military.com/daily-news/2012/08/09/army-adapts-to-post-afghanistan-mission.html (accessed 22 August 2012).

for major combat operations? The decision to decrease the fighting force, Brigade Combat Teams, from 45 to 32 will also decrease the capability as well. According to President Obama, the military needs to train for every possible threat and contingency. "Yes, our military will be leaner, but the world must know–the United States is going to maintain our military superiority with armed forces that are agile, flexible and ready for the full range of contingencies and threats."[163]

In summary, leaders present decisions focused on cancelling programs for technical equipment. In addition, these decisions to reduce the size of the force diminish the possible capability leaders may apply to potential problems. As the current environment illustrates, decisions have reduced our resources: our technology programs, combat focused training and a reduction in the capacity, possibly causing a disparity between the total numbers and the mission. The leaders' current decisions may be thrusting our military toward another hollow force.

Conclusions

In 1980, General Meyer coined the phrase hollow forces, which to him meant the lack of adequate personnel.[164] From the moment Meyer stated that phrase before a Congressional hearing, people of all sorts (politicians, military leaders, journalists, and others) warned against a hollow force or disputed its very existence. Analyzing case studies show how technology, training, and numbers have led to the perception of hollow forces. The literature review of this document showed that several authors including both Mr. Richard Betts and General Meyer meant different things when they spoke of hollow forces. The phrase, hollow force remains elusive due to a lack of understanding. Authors cited different examples for potential causes of a hollow force. One could argue, such as Meyer, that forces which lacked manning are hollow.

---

[163]John T. Bennett, "Obama Announces New Military Strategy," *The Hill*, 5 January 2012, http://thehill.com/blogs/defcon-hill/policy-and-strategy/202505-new-pentagon-strategy-ends-plan-to-fight-two-wars-at-once (accessed 22 August 2012).

[164] The author deduced this from General Meyer's testimony regarding the lack of personnel filling out units.

However, one must ask the question, "Why are forces with low manning hollow?" If a force with insufficient manning accomplishes the assigned mission, is the force hollow?

Table 1.   Findings within Case Studies

Hollow Force Case Study	Lack of Technology	Lack of Training	Lack of Numbers
Korean War	Yes	Yes	Yes
After Vietnam	No	Yes	Yes
After Cold War	No	No	No
Present Conflict	Yes	Yes	Yes
Yes = variable present in case study No = variable not present in case study			

Source: Created by author.

With the fortunate record of accomplishment of the United States Armed Forces following the Vietnam War to the present day, many continue to argue that a hollow force simply does not exist and it is only one's perception. However, as the case studies illustrate hollow forces did exist due to lack of training and numbers (see Table 1) following World War II, during the Korean War, and after Vietnam, during the failed rescue attempt in Iran, and in Grenada. Following the Cold War however, the case study illustrates no hollow force, most likely due to numbers and training that occurred in preparation for the possible attack by the Soviet Union. The reduction process following the Cold War had not decreased forces to the point of creating a hollow force. The last case study observing the present day illustrates ideal conditions for a hollow force.

Leaders must grapple with the amount of "hollowness" or unreadiness the nation can afford. According to Richard Betts in his book, *Military Readiness: Concepts, Choices,*

Consequences, "Getting the answer wrong exacts a price in one currency or the other: either in blood in wartime or in treasure in peacetime.[165]

Recommendations

Following the analysis of the case studies, one can appreciate the relationship between strategic choices, resources, and hollow forces. Below are suggestions to circumvent hollow forces:

1. Avoid using the term "hollow forces" altogether and focus rather on military readiness. Since its inception by General Meyer, people altered the meaning significantly causing confusion during discussion.

2. Civilian leaders must consider other alternatives to complete missions than assigning them to reduced number of forces. Smaller forces, although may become more efficient, may not have sufficient numbers to accomplish assigned missions.

3. Leaders must consider forces that have trained for the type of mission assigned. Operational leaders must train forces on the most difficult task which may be assigned by civilian leadership.

---

[165]Betts, *Military Readiness Concepts, Choices, Consequences*, 32.

Bibliography

Books

Betts, Richard K. *Military Readiness Concepts, Choices, Consequences*. Washington, DC: The Brookings Institution, 1995.

Bourque, Stephen. *JAYHAWK! The Seventh Corps in the Persian Gulf War*. Washington, DC: Department of the Army, 2002.

Clausewitz, Carl von. *On War*. Translated and Edited by Michael Howard and Peter Paret. Princeton, NJ: Princeton University Press, 1976.

Fehrenbach, T. R. *This Kind of War: A Study in Unpreparedness*. New York: The Macmillan Company, 1963.

Finlan, Alistair. *The Gulf War 1991: Essential Histories*. Great Britain: Osprey Publishing, 2003.

Griffith, Robert K. *The US Army's Transition to the All-Volunteer Force 1968-1974*. Washington, DC: Center of Military History, Unites States Army, 1997.

Headquarters, Department of the Army. Army Regulation 220-1, *Army Unit Status Reporting and Force Registration-Consolidated Policies*. Washington, DC: Government Printing Office, 2010.

———. Field Manual 5-0, Change 1, *The Operations Process*. Washington, DC: Government Printing Office, 2011.

Henderson, William Darryl. *The Hollow Army*. New York: Greenwood Press, 1990.

Joint Chiefs of Staff. Joint Publication 1-02, *Department of Defense Dictionary of Military and Associated Terms*. Washington, DC: Government Printing Office, 8 November 2010 (as amended through 15 January 2012).

Mendez, M. Albert, and Lee Russell, Illustrated by Paul Hannon. *Granada 1983*. Great Britain: Osprey Publishing Ltd, 1985.

O'Hanlon, Michael E. *The Science of War*. Princeton, NJ: Princeton University Press, 2009.

Turabian, Kate L. *A Manual for Writers of Research Papers, Theses, and Dissertations*. 7th ed. Chicago: University of Chicago Press, 2007.

U.S. Congress. House. *National Defense Funding Levels for Fiscal Year 1981: Hearing before the Investigations Subcommittee of the Committee on Armed Services*. Washington, DC: Government Printing Office, 1980.

Van Evera, Stephen. *Guide to Methods for Students of Political Science*. Ithaca, NY: Cornell University Press, 1997.

On-line Resources

American Enterprise Institute, Foreign Policy Initiative, and The Heritage Foundation. "Defending Defense Warning Hollow Force Ahead! The Effect of Ever More Defense Budget Cuts on U.S. Armed Forces." 21 July 2011. http://www.heritage.org/research/ reports/2011/07/defending-defense-warning-hollow-force-ahead (accessed 22 August 2012).

Aspin, Les. "Bottom-Up-Review." October 1993. http://www.fas.org/man/docs/bur/part04.htm (accessed 22 August 2012).

Bacon, Lance M. "Odierno: Brigade Cuts Needed to Reorganize." *Army Times*, 3 March 2012. http://www.armytimes.com/news/2012/03/army-ray-odierno-says-brigade-combat-team-cuts-needed-reorganize-030312w/ (accessed 22 August 2012).

Bennett, John T. "Obama Announces New Military Strategy." *The Hill*, 5 January 2012. http://thehill.com/blogs/defcon-hill/policy-and-strategy/202505-new-pentagon-strategy-ends-plan-to-fight-two-wars-at-once (accessed 22 August 2012).

Bloomer, Charles. "America's hollow army." posted 10 April 2000. http://www.enterstage right.com/archive/articles/0400military.htm (accessed 22 August 2012).

Bowman, Michael. "Obama Administration Defends Afghanistan Timeline." voanews.com, 27 May 2012. http://www.voanews.com/content/obama_administration_defends_ afghanistan_withdrawal_timeline/1105882.html (accessed 22 August 2012).

Bumiller, Elisabeth, and Thom Shanker. "In New Strategy, Panetta Plans Even Smaller Army." *New York Times*, 5 January 2012. http://www.nytimes.com/2012/01/05/us/in-new-strategy-panetta-plans-even-smaller-army.html (accessed 22 August 2012).

Caratano, James. "How to Grade a "Hollow" Military." Heritage Network. 7 February 2012. http://blog.heritage.org/2012/02/07/how-to-grade-a-hollow-military/. (accessed 22 August 2012).

Congressional Budget Office. "Trends in Selected Indicators of Military Readiness, 1980 Through 1993." Washington, DC: CBO Papers, March 1994. http://www.cbo.gov/sites/default/files/cbofiles/ftpdocs/48xx/doc4888/doc13.pdf (accessed 22 August 2012).

Cox, Matthew. "Army Adapts to Post-Afghanistan Mission." 9 August 2012. http://www.military.com/daily-news/2012/08/09/army-adapts-to-post-afghanistan-mission.html (accessed 22 August 2012).

Daggett, Stephen, and Andrew Feickert. *A Historical Perspective on "Hollow Forces"*. Washington, DC: Congressional Research Service, 2012. http://www.fas.org/sgp/crs/natsec/R42334.pdf (accessed 22 August 2012).

Eaglen, Mackenzie. "Military Already Being Cut, But Obama Makes It Official." *The Foundry*, 13 April 2011. http://blog.heritage.org/2011/04/13/military-already-being-cut-but-obama-makes-it-official/ (accessed 22 August 2012).

Erwin, Sandra I. "Cries of 'Hollow Military' Stifle Rational Debate on Future Spending." *National Defense*, June 2011. http://www.nationaldefensemagazine.org/archive/2011/ June/Pages/Criesof%E2%80%98HollowMilitary%E2%80%99StifleRationalDebateonFut ureSpending.aspx (accessed 22 August 2012).

Headquarters, Department of the Army. Field Manual (FM) 3-24, *Counterinsurgency*. Washington, DC: Government Printing Office, December 2006. http://www.fas.org/irp/doddir/army/fm3-24.pdf (accessed 22 August 2012).

GlobalSecurity.org. "Brigade Unit of Action." http://www.globalsecurity.org/military/ agency/army/bua.htm (accessed 22 August 2012).

———. "US Army 1990 Divisions." http://www.globalsecurity.org/military/ agency/army/division-90.htm (accessed 22 August 2012).

Graham, Owen. "Armed Forces Face Major Cuts in Budget." Posted 21 August 2012. http://www.vindy.com/news/2012/aug/21/armed-forces-face-major-cuts-in-budgets/?newswatch (accessed 22 August 2012).

Infoplease. "Active Duty Personnel." http://www.infoplease.com/ipa/A0004598.html (accessed 22 August 2012).

Kaufmann, William W. "Hollow Forces? Current Issues of U.S. Military Readiness and Effectiveness." *The Brookings Review* (December 1994): 24-29. http://www.unz.org/Pub/BrookingsRev-1994q4-00024 (accessed 22 August 2012).

Kitfield, James. "The Myth of the Hollow Force." *Government Executive*, 14 December 1998. http://www.govexec.com/federal-news/1998/12/the-myth-of-the-hollow-force/5300/ (accessed 22 August 2012).

Meinhart, Richard. "Strategic Planning by the Chairmen, Joint Chiefs of Staff, 1990 to 2005." Monograph, Strategic Studies Institute, April 2006. http://www.comw.org/ qdr/fulltext/0604meinhart.pdf (accessed 22 August 2012).

Military Factory. "Sikorsky CH-53 Sea Lion Heavy-Lift Transport Helicopter." Last updated 5 February 2011. http://www.militaryfactory.com/aircraft/detail.asp?aircraft_id=178 (accessed 22 August 2012).

Mullen, M. G., Admiral U.S. Navy. "CJCS Guidance 2011." http://www.jcs.mil/content/ files/2011-01/011011165132_CJCS_Annual_Guidance_2011.pdf (accessed 22 August 2012).

PBS. Frontline: Chronology the Gulf War. http://www.pbs.org/wgbh/pages/frontline/gulf/cron/. (accessed 22 August 2012).

Petraeus, General David H. "Military Farewell Retirement Address." *American Rhetoric Online Speech Bank*. Delivered 31 August 2011, Arlington, VA. http://www.american rhetoric.com/speeches/davidpetraeusretirementspeech.htm (accessed 22 August 2012).

RAND Corporation. "The Evolution of the All-Volunteer Force." Research Brief, 2006. http://www.rand.org/pubs/research_briefs/RB9195/index1.html (accessed 22 August 2012).

Schmitt, Eric. "Troops Queries Leave Rumsfeld on the Defensive." *New York Times*, 9 December 2004. http://www.nytimes.com/2004/12/09/international/middleeast/09rumsfeld.html (accessed 22 August 2012).

Tice, Jim. "Earlier Drawdowns Give Idea of What Is to Come." *Army Forum*. http://www.armytimes.com/news/2012/02/army-earlier-drawdowns-give-idea-whats-to-come-021912w/ (accessed 22 August 2012).

Tristam, Pierre. "The Failed Rescue of American Hostages in Iran on April 24, 1980." About.com. Middle East Issues. http://middleeast.about.com/od/usmideastpolicy/ a/me090413b.htm (accessed 22 August 2012).

———. "What was Operation Eagle Claw, the Failed Rescue of American Hostages in Iran?" About.com. Middle East Issues. http://middleeast.about.com/od/usmideastpolicy/ f/me090413c.htm (accessed 22 August 2012).

U.S. Department of Defense. *Quadrennial Defense Review Report*. Washington, DC, February 2010. http://www.defense.gov/qdr/qdr%20as%20of%2029jan10%201600.PDF (accessed 22 August 2012).

———. *Sustaining U.S. Global Leadership: Priorities for 21st Century Defense*. Washington, DC: January 2012. http://www.defense.gov/news/Defense_Strategic_Guidance.pdf (accessed 22 August 2012).

U.S. Senate. Subcommittee on Readiness and Management Support Committee on Armed Services. *Hearing to Receive Testimony on the Current Readiness of U.S. Forces in Review of the Defense Authorization Request for Fiscal Year 2013 and the Future Years Defense Program.* Washington, DC: 10 May 2012. http://armed-services.senate.gov/ Transcripts/2012/05%20May/12-37%20-%205-10-12.pdf (accessed 22 August 2012).

Ziemke, Earl F. *Army Historical Series: The U.S. Army in the Occupation of Germany 1944-1946.* http://www.history.army.mil/books/wwii/Occ-GY/ch18.htm#b1 (accessed 22 August 2012).